MW01290216

THE POWER OF
"I"

(10 Inspirational Lessons)
Conquering Life's Challenges and
Embracing Who You Are!

COACH REGGIE WARD

XULON PRESS

Xulon Press
2301 Lucien Way #415
Maitland, FL 32751
407.339.4217
www.xulonpress.com

Unless otherwise indicated, Scripture quotations taken
from the King James Version (KJV) – *public domain*.

Printed in the United States of America

Paperback ISBN-13: 978-1-66283-349-6
Hard Cover ISBN-13:978-1-66283-350-2
Ebook ISBN-13:978-1-66283-351-9

THE INSPIRATIONAL CONTENTS

Dedication

This book is dedicated to
my wonderful, beautiful and beloved mother…
Mary Elizabeth Ward

<u>"A Mother's Prayer"</u>

Dear Heavenly Father, thank you for this day, thank you
my Family and thank you
for blessing me.

Lord, I pray for my Mother
I pray for a Spirit of healing and strength
A Mother's love is precious, kind, loving and everlasting.

She listens, she's open, she's thoughtful. She's giving of
herself beyond measure and......
She is always available and accessible for her children
and others.

So Lord, I thank you for giving me an example of your
goodness, mercy and grace.

I Love You Mom
from your
Loving Son Reggie

THE BEGINNING...

The "I" in *The Power of "I"* stands for inspiration. *The Power of "I"* is the inspirational blueprint for you to manage emotions, make sound decisions, and overcome the challenges of life. John L. Buckley once said, "Most people don't Plan to Fail, they simply Fail to Plan."[1]. This is a profound statement that many recognize and, thus, we set up plans. These plans will normally feature a financial plan to manage and understand money, an educational plan to increase knowledge and awareness, and a nutritional plan to improve health and fitness.

These plans are substantial in building good lives for us but fall short of the mark for many to live complete lives. They do not prepare for life's unexpected changes, conflict with others, bad relationships, disagreements with loved ones, or even self-doubt. Many people seldom speak about the value of managing emotions and dealing with the challenges of life. But if you do include inspiration in your life plan, it provides inner strength, clarifies your mindset, and most of all, completes the mark of maximizing your ability to cope with life's ups and downs.

The Power of "I" is the driving force to educate, inspire, and give courage to people for handling difficult problems. As a result, by adding this inspirational plan to your life, you will live a more decisive, prepared, and complete life. *The Power of "I"* is designed to solve problems, overcome life's difficulties, and give confidence to live your dreams. Now, go, use what you learn, and be who you are called to be.

"Begin doing what you want to do now. We are not living in eternity. We have only this moment, sparkling like a star in our hand and melting like a snowflake." — M.B. Ray[2]

My Inspiration is...

My Faith
My Family
My Passion to Help Others
My Brothers of Notre Dame: (B.O.N.D.)

Special Thanks to the Women in My Life

Mary E. Ward & Coach Reggie Ward

My wife Rhonda, who showed me the importance of love,
caring for others, and listening.
My mother Mary, who taught me the meaning of sacrifice,
loyalty, and believing in myself.
My sister Gina, who showed me the value of friendship,
favor, and trust.
My granddaughter Paytin, who reminds me of innocence
and gives me hope for the future.

The Ultimate Lesson Lives and Breathes in You!

"No matter what kind of challenges or difficulties or painful situations you go through in your life, we all have something deep within us that we can reach down and find the inner strength to get through them." Alana Stewart[3]

Let's begin this journey by uncovering the meaning of inspiration. Inspiration is defined in Webster's Dictionary as "stimulation of the mind or emotions to a high level of activity or feeling...releasing divine influence of man's mind and soul."[4] Inspiration can be found in various aspects of life: music, stories, speeches, and people. The following ten lessons will lay out the inspirational plan and its foundation, which is based on the questions of why, who, what, when, where, and how. This fundamental question approach is the cornerstone for the Inspirational Alphabet, its process, and the future. Inspiration is the ultimate lesson of life. Inspiration represents that uncompromising quality that is limitless, powerful, divine, and it lives and breathes in you!

PART I.

"THE FOUNDATION IS IN THE WHY & WHO"

LESSON 1:

THE VALUE IS IN THE "I"

"Your ordinary acts of love and hope,
point to the extraordinary promise that
every human life is of inestimable value."
Desmond Tutu[5]

Inspiration is important because it is a reminder of all our hope in life. Sometimes life changes for the better: marriage, career advancement, and improved financial position. But sometimes life changes for the worse: job loss, divorce, or close friend who passes, and thus it is inevitable you have to deal with each of these changes. So what better way to deal with change than through inspiration? Inspiration is the emotional connection, the feeling in your heart that gives you the power to believe and have courage to act and ability to conquer life's challenges.

Motivational speaker Tony Robbins says, "Only those who have learned the power of sincere and selfless contribution experience life's deepest joy: true fulfillment."[6] You have the essence of inspiration, and it lives and breathes in you. You have to display a positive attitude, beliefs, and commitment to allow yourself to be who you are while dealing with successes, challenges, and unforeseen circumstances of life. The answer to why inspiration is important is simple. Life will be tough, so you will need to remind yourself that you have the energy, hope, and grit to defeat hard times and live out your dreams.

LESSON 2:

THE SPECIAL INGREDIENT

"Do your little of good where you are: it's
those little bits of good put together that
overwhelm the world." Desmond Tutu[7]

Many aspects of life need inspiration—for example,
children, families, friendships, relationships, businesses, and the list goes on and on. All you need is a little
something special to have success. But what is truly invaluable is the actual word "need." Need is defined as "essential
or something required, like food, water and shelter are the
necessities of life."[8]

However, to achieve goals and dreams and handle the
challenges of life, inspiration adds the special ingredient to
push you through the next level. Everyone needs inspiration, especially those who live with severe problems—for
example, a single parent dealing with children, job loss, and
stress; the teenager choosing friends, knowing who to trust,
and how to deal with personal appearance. When facing
these challenges, you must call on your essential inspiration

to make clear decisions, create positive changes, and become a better person.

Part II.

"The What & the When are Life's True Rewards"

Lesson 3:

Rewards are Inevitable

"Each day provides its own gifts."
Marcus Aurelius[9]

Rewards are gifts because each day provide opportunities to grow, love, and inspire. Inspiration unleashes personal rewards of self-confidence, resilience, strength, boldness, self-esteem, and humility in people. The rewards of inspiration are limitless, timeless, and plentiful to handle life's challenges and help you become who you are. Inspiration gives you determination to pursue your dreams when no one believes in you. Inspiration provides you with a relentless belief that sees beyond the things you cannot control: layoffs, relationships, and even dealing with death. But inspiration's most powerful measure is its capacity to open and expand your mind's potential. This capacity releases creativity and exceptional strength to achieve more than what you think you can while also showing what you are capable of becoming. Once these rewards spring into action, the possibilities are endless to conquer problems and discover the magic inside of you.

Lesson 4:

Raising Your Game

"When you get into a tight place and everything goes against you, till it seems as though you could not hang on a minute longer, never give up then, for that is just the place and time the tide will turn."
Harriet Beecher Stowe[10]

Inspiration is needed each and every day because you are faced with making decisions every day, but it is most needed during life's challenges, during times of self-doubt, and in difficult situations. Life is filled with complex obstacles, difficult people, and multiple problems that require more of you. Here are some key examples of adversity that people encounter; I call these challenges the real deal.

Parents dealing with teenagers growing up, talking back, and not respecting authority; coaches dealing with players that do not follow instruction, listen, and/or don't understand the importance of teamwork. In addition, children dealing with opinions of controlling parents and their expectations along with choices about education and friendships; employees dealing with demanding bosses, deadlines, employee relations, and financial pressures. These real-deal experiences are fundamental life situations that make you wonder, can I really handle all of this? Is this what life is all about, or is there a plan to manage this craziness?

Inspiration is the plan to help and is essential to uncover hope, provide clarity to make decisions with relationships, set goals, and make career choices. As a result, inspiration is that extra sense, that internal quality for you to prepare, to move forward, and to thrive throughout life, especially during troublesome times.

PART III.

"THE WHERE & THE HOW...
UNCOVER THE PLAN"

LESSON 5:

TOUCHES THE HEART

"Everyone has inside of him a piece of good news. The good news is that you don't know how great you can be! How much you can love!!! What you can accomplish! And what your potential is!" Anne Frank[11]

As you continue to learn more about "The Power of I," you can understand that inspiration may come from various areas of life. Sometimes it comes from good experiences: marriage, career promotions, and great investment decisions. On the contrary, sometimes it comes from bad experiences: past relationships, loss of career, or death of a loved one. But for this lesson, let's focus on the areas that touch our minds and spirits. There are three areas that can explain where inspiration touches the hearts and minds of us all through bold quotes, scriptures, and songs. Quotes can remind you of your gifts and talents: "I am The Greatest"—Muhammad Ali,[12] "The Separation is in the Preparation"—Russell Wilson[13] "We can be the Drivers of our Destiny" —Peter Arnell.[14]

Scriptures provide lessons to balance and enhance the quality of life. "For as much is given much is required" (Luke 12:48); "Let your light shine"[1](Matt. 5:16); and "For with God nothing is impossible"[16] (Luke 1:23). Songs are the harmonious connections to what you feel in mind, body, and soul: "The Greatest Love of All" by George Benson [15], "Pray" by Ce-Ce Winans [16], and "Shining Star" by Earth, Wind & Fire [17].

These are three very influential areas of life that can help you understand where the power of inspiration lives; it may be words, scriptures, and songs. This inspiration plan releases creativity, provides uniqueness, and helps you embrace your true self. Therefore, as you go through life, remember life is full of a variety of challenges, and to handle these situations, your inspirational plan needs diversity. Words, scriptures, and songs are not the only ways to handle emotions and problems but can help inspire you to focus and believe in being the best you can be. This represents the powerful answer to the question where does inspiration come? ...YOU.

LESSON 6:

THE Y.O.C: YOU, OTHERS & COMMUNITY

> "Start by what is necessary; then do what's possible; and suddenly you are doing the impossible. "Francis of Assisi[18]

Inspiration can be used three ways: 1) to motivate yourself; 2) to encourage others; and 3) to galvanize a community. Let's take a closer look at how inspiration is used in today's world. You can use inspiration to motivate yourself to accomplish a goal, to stay focused on priorities, and to live a better life. You can use inspiration to encourage others by listening to them, by accepting them, and by being their friend. Lastly, inspiration can enhance a community by reminding people of the good times—for example, when businesses are prosperous; when children are happy playing, learning, and thriving; and, most importantly, when families are growing and building for the future. Inspiration is a ray of light that strengthens your actions, promotes goodness, and ignites people to live full lives filled with love, honor, and hope.

PART IV.

"THE EDGE" IS YOUR ABC'S

Lesson 7:

The Inspirational Alphabet

"Everything should be made as Simple as possible, but not Simpler." Albert Einstein[19]

The Inspirational Alphabet is designed using the fundamentals of learning, our alphabet. Our alphabet is simple, clear, and relatable. This inspirational model is a list of your gifts and talents. Each letter is defined two ways to inspire who you are and who you are to become. The first part will be a quality associated with the letter, and the second will give a positive statement to help you make choices when experiencing difficult and troubled times. As you read the Inspirational Alphabet, begin with each letter and say to yourself, "I am" and then say the word. For example, "I am amazing!"

A—Approachable, Adaptive, Available, Amazing

"Be amazing today."

B—Brave, Breathtaking, Belief

"Always believe in yourself."

C— Confident, Commitment, Consistent, Caring

"Commit to your dreams."

D—Decisive, Determined, Discipline, Driven

"Always be decisive."

E—Enthusiastic, Engaging, Excellent, Encouraging

"Enthusiasm is infectious."

F—Faithful, Forgiving, Focused, Flexible

"Remember to forgive."

G—Goodness, Grateful, Giving, Gifted, Goal-Oriented

"Give to others."

H—Humble, Honorable, Happy, Hopeful

"Remember to honor and appreciate your father and mother."

I—Integrity, Intelligent, Intensity

"Integrity is the light of your soul."

J—Joyous, Jubilant, Jesus

"Joy is in your heart."

K—Kind, Knowledgeable

"Kindness costs you nothing."

L— Loving

"Love is the most powerful gift in the world."

M—Motivated, Mentally Tough, Masterful

"Have the right mindset."

N—New, Now, Noble

"Every day is a new opportunity."

O—Open, Obedient, Ownership

"Own your choices."

P—Peace, Patient, Prayerful, Purposeful, Punctual

"Patience builds strength."

Q—Quiet

"There is peace in quietness."

R—Righteous, Respectful, Reliable, Ready

"Do what is right."

S—Spirit-Filled, Strong, Self-Control, Serving

"Self-control provides protection of mind, body, and soul."

T—Thankful, Timely, Talented, Tough, Trustworthy

"Always say thank you."

U—Unique, Understanding, Unyielding

"Unity grows the community."

V—Valuable, Victorious, Vibrant

"Victory is defined by you and only you."

W—Willing, Wonderful

"Be willing."

X—X-Factor— God-given talents designed ONLY for you!

"You are forever connected with God"

Y—You

"You are a superstar."

Z—Zealous (Passion)

"Your zeal elevates your destiny."

The Inspirational Alphabet keeps life as simple as A, B, C. It holds a monumental impact on how to respond while managing emotions, making decisions, and going through life's journey. The letter and the encouragement statement associated with the letter show how to handle the ups and downs of life. The combination of these two methods creates an inspirational strategy. The Inspirational Alphabet not only prepares you for the challenges of life but provides a unique platform to make quality choices for yourself and live as a shining example for others to follow.

PART V.

"The Ultimate Power"

Lesson 8:

Your Name Stands Alone

"What Lies in behind you and what lies in front of you, pales in comparison to what lies inside of you." Ralph Waldo Emerson[20]

Your name is your birthright! It identifies you with your family, your history, and your community. Your name provides the intrinsic meaning of who you are, what you stand for, and how you will ultimately influence future generations. For example, my name Reginald means "mighty advisor, kingly and counselor." Once you realize the meaning of your name, you will begin to live in alignment with your true purpose as this realization will unveil the power of inspiration. Challenge yourself to seek the meaning of your name, to know who you are, and then use your life to inspire others.

LESSON 9:

THE INSPIRATION SYSTEM

"The best and most beautiful things in the world cannot be seen or even touched-they must be felt in the heart." Helen Keller[21]

Each and every one of us has his/her own inspiration plan, and it lives and breathes in our hearts. Many of us need a way, process, or plan to release it but simply do not understand how to touch the source. This inspiration guide allows you to uncover and release your power to live your purpose. To truly fulfill your dreams, goals, and destiny, you must tap into your inspiration plan. Below is a "seven-step process" that, when combined with your dreams, will lift you to ultimate success.

Below is the 7- Step Inspirational Blueprint:

1. Name your goal/dream and/or situation you are currently experiencing.

2. Spell your name vertically on a sheet of paper.

3. Review the Inspiration Alphabet.

4. Write down each word and life statement connected with each letter of your name.

5. Summarize and write your Inspiration Plan using the "will"—see below.

6. Keep your inspirational plan visible.

7. Add this to your life plan, apply to each goal, and go after them!

Example:

My Inspiration Plan

Goal: Impact lives

Name: Reginald

R: Righteous - "Do the right thing."

E: Enthusiastic - "Enthusiasm is infectious."

G: Giving - "Give to others."

I: Integrity - "Integrity is the light of the soul."

N: New - "Everything is new."

A: Amazing - "Be amazing today."

L: Love - "Love is the most powerful word in the world."

D: Discipline - "Be decisive and diligent."

In the example above, the name R.E.G.I.N.A.L.D portrays how each person is born with his/her own unique Inspirational Plan. The Inspirational Plan reads... **"Reginald is righteous, and I will thrive to do the right thing. I will approach life with an infectious enthusiasm. I will... give to others, represent integrity, and be a beacon of light. Reginald will treat everything new and say to himself 'I will be amazing today.' I will embrace the most powerful word in the world, love, to be the best man that I can be with family, friends, and the community. Lastly, I will make choices using compassion, decisiveness, and diligence."** Your name creates the ultimate power that is unveiled through a personal statement of confidence, built to handle the challenges of life and surpass any and all expectations.

This Inspirational Alphabet is incredible! It is filled with quality lessons and provides an extraordinary personal mission statement. The Inspirational Alphabet is the simple but powerful platform to make decisions while keeping a positive mindset. These dynamic attributes of your name are compiled, uniquely arranged, and designed fitting you and only you. The Inspirational Alphabet recognizes and shows that each person's birthright contains unique gifts and talents to be strong, courageous, and able to deal with life. Now, it is your turn to use this Inspirational Alphabet to develop your own mission statement to conquer life's challenges with hope, strength, and power.

PART VI.

"The Inspirational Call to Action"

LESSON 10:

THE FUTURE IS NOW

"Begin doing what you do now. We are not living in eternity. We have only this moment, sparkling like a star in our hand and melting like a snowflake." M.B. Ray

*T*he Power of "I" is a guide to educate, inspire, and handle problems and to make quality decisions. The Inspirational Plan utilizes the alphabet model as a reminder that life is very simple. In this simplicity, power is unveiled, goals are achieved, and, most importantly, you have the strength to leave a legacy. *The Power of "I"* is a call to action to be who you are, to challenge you, and to apply the lessons to your life.

The "Why" in inspiration is a reminder of all the good things in life. The "Who" is a reminder that all people need inspiration to always have hope and optimize life. The "What" allows you to achieve more than what you are capable of in life. The "When" in inspiration is needed each and every day because you are faced with challenges and making decisions. The "Where" in inspiration comes from people, places, songs, and experiences, good and bad, but true inspiration comes from you. The "How" in inspiration can be used three ways: 1) to motivate yourself, 2) to encourage others, and 3) to galvanize a community.

The Power of "I" is your unique source of strength, power, and courage. As you continue your journey, it will inspire you to release your gifts and talents. Always remember you are enough...and inspiration comes from many aspects of life. But, ultimately, its truth lies in the person that you see in the mirror each and every day...YOU!

SOURCES OF INSPIRATIONS

QUOTES:

"I am The Greatest"—Muhammad Ali-World Champion Professional Boxer

"Preparation Builds Separation" —Russell Wilson-NFL Super Bowl Champion-FB-Quarterback

"We Can be the Drivers of our Destiny"—Peter Arnell, Branding & Design Expert

"Every man should have P.R.I.D.E.-Personal, Responsibility in Daily Excellence" [22]—Lou Holtz, Hall of Fame Football Coach

"It's about moving forward, not looking backward and changing for the better and forever." Martha Stewart [23]- American Business Woman

Scriptures:

Responsibility: "For as much is given, much is required." (Luke 12:48)

Purpose: "For all things work together for good, for those who love the Lord who are called according to his purpose." (Romans 8:28)

Self-Control: "He that has no rule over his own spirit is like a city that is broken down and without walls." (Proverbs 25:28)

Daily Living: "The steps of a good man are ordered by the Lord: and he delighteth in his way. " (Psalm 37:23)

Faith: "For with God nothing shall be impossible." (Luke 1:37)

Life: "Let your light shine." (Matthew 5:16)

Testimonials:

What People are Saying about Coach Reggie:

I. Cris Tenorio:

> "At our first meeting, Reggie exuded the sense that he is a man with a character to serve others. He is approachable with a spirit of patience and understanding and imparts wisdom that gives direction. Finally, he is motivational, which has been a key part to our family relationship that aligns with our values and belief systems to journey with us to the next level. Thank you for your unconditional love toward us."

II. Cherry Buckle:

> "Reggie has been an amazing influence on my daughter, Brianna. He taught her the importance of believing in herself and to be humble in all she does. Throughout the last few years, I have seen her confidence flourish both in and out of the pool. Reggie has helped Brianna tremendously with the

transition from being a high school athlete to competing at the collegiate level. We are so grateful to have Reggie as a part of our daughter's journey.

Good luck with your book!"

III. Tony Saenz:

"My son, Jake Saenz, began his athletic and life training with Coach Reggie at age seven. For the past two years, Coach Ward has developed and increased his playing performance with football and baseball. This has included his speed and agility, strength, hitting and catching, fielding, and field vision for football. Coach Ward also instills hard work on and off the field, responsibility for your actions, good ethics, and faith! Thank you, Coach Reggie Ward."

IV. Ronice Thomas:

"On behalf of our family, we are indebted to Coach Reggie and the abilities he has developed and cultivated in my son. Because of you, my son has found his true calling. I justly believe he will do an illimitable amount of good in this world as he sets forth to accomplish his goal to someday play professional baseball. As we reflect on my son's countless years of engaging in organized sports, there is a particular year that stands out most.

"The year my son was effectively taught how to swing for accuracy to someday 'hit that home run'; the year my son was allowed to unapologetically show his strengths to take charge and remind the bases of who was in control; and lastly, the year my son cherished a coach that not only mirrored him but believed my son was capable of anything he challenged his mind to do. So, because of this year, we congratulate you, Coach Reggie, for your mentorship. I trust you have left an unforgettable impression on my son, and for that, you are truly one of a kind!

Wishing you continued success."

ABOUT
THE AUTHOR

Coach Reginald "Reggie" Ward has dedicated over 35 years of his life to athletics and serving his community. Whether that be playing, coaching, mentoring or volunteering he loves helping young people realize their dreams. During this journey there has been many successes and failures.

There are tremendous learnings in both experiences, but the greatest learning comes from the failures. You must endure the pain, you must overcome the difficulties and power through the challenges of life. The results are life-long lessons building strength, perseverance, humility and confidence.

Coach Reggie has decided to write, to share, to inspire and provide a plan to conquer life's challenges. Bottom line, he is simply fulfilling the appointment... "To Learn, To Go Forth and To Serve" given to him by his alma mater... Long Beach Poly High School- "Home of Scholars and Champions".

Now go, take- action and live your destiny!!

RESOURCES

I.   Internet

Stewart, Alana-

https://www.brainyquote.com/quotes/alana_stewart_712676

Inspirational Quotes, http://quotes.com/topics/Inspirational quotes

(Section S) Brainy Quotes, assessed May 30, 2020, Xplore, 2001

Ray, M.B.

https://susandorling.wordpress.com/tag/quotes-by-m-b-ray/

Inspirational Quotes, http://quotes.com/topics/Inspirational quotes (Section R)

Brainy Quotes, assessed May 30, 2020, Xplore, 2001

Tutu, Desmond-

https://www.brainyquote.com/quotes/desmond_tutu_454152

https://www.brainyquote.com/quotes/desmond_tutu_387490

Inspirational Quotes, http://quotes.com/topics/Inspirational quotes (Section T)

Brainy Quotes, assessed May 30, 2020, Xplore, 2001

Aurelius, Marcus-

https://www.brainyquote.com/quotes/marcus_aurelius_380330

Inspirational Quotes, http://quotes.com/topics/Inspirational quotes

(Section A) Brainy Quotes, assessed May 30, 2020, Xplore, 2001

Stowe, Harriet Beecher-

https://www.brainyquote.com/quotes/harriet_beecher_stowe_126390

Inspirational Quotes, http://quotes.com/topics/Inspirational quotes (Section S) Brainy Quotes, assessed May 30, 2020, Xplore, 2001

Robbins, Tony-

https://www.brainyquote.com/quotes/tony_robbins_147769

Inspirational Quotes, http://quotes.com/topics/Inspirational
quotes (Section R)

Brainy Quotes, assessed May 30, 2020, Xplore, 2001

Frank Anne-

https://www.brainyquote.com/quotes/anne_frank_121214

Inspirational Quotes, http://quotes.com/topics/Inspirational
quotes (Section F)

Brainy Quotes, assessed May 30, 2020, Xplore, 2001

Assisi, Francis of-

https://www.brainyquote.com/quotes/francis_of_assisi_121023

Inspirational   Quotes,   http://quotes.com/topics/
Inspirational quotes

(Section A) Brainy Quotes, assessed May 30, 2020, Xplore, 2001

Einstein, Albert-

https://www.brainyquote.com/quotes/albert_einstein_103652

Inspirational Quotes, http://quotes.com/topics/Inspirational
quotes (Section E)

Brainy Quotes, assessed May 30, 2020, Xplore, 2001

Emerson, Ralph Waldo-

h t t p s : / / w w w . b r a i n y q u o t e . c o m / q u o t e s /
ralph_waldo_emerson_386697

Inspirational Quotes, http://quotes.com/topics/Inspirational
quotes (Section E) Brainy Quotes, assessed May 30, 2020,
Xplore, 2001

Keller Helen,-

https://www.brainyquote.com/quotes/helen_keller_101301

Inspirational Quotes, http://quotes.com/topics/Inspirational
quotes (Section K)

Brainy Quotes, assessed May 30, 2020, Xplore, 2001

Dyer, Wayne-

https://www.brainyquote.com/quotes/wayne_dyer_718093

Inspirational Daily Quotes, http://quotes.com/topics/
Inspirational quotes (Section D) Inspirational Daily Quotes,
assessed May 30, 2020,

Wilson Russell-

https://www.pinterest.com/pin/18647785931867236/

Inspirational Quotes, http:/pinterest.com/topics/ Inspirational quotes

(Section Russell Wilson)," Preparation Builds Separation", assessed May 30, 2020

Holtz Lou, 2013

http://jayposick.blogspot.com/2013/03/

'Personal Responsibility in Daily Excellence P.R.I.D.E'

http://www.Jayposick.blogspot.com

Jay' Journal: 3/28/2013, P.R.I.D.E,

assessed May 30,2020

Ali -Muhammad Ali- '30 of Muhammad Ali's best quotes'

https://www.usatoday.com/story/sports/boxing/2016/06/03/ muhammad-ali-best-quotes-boxing/85370850/

http://www.usa.com,USA Today Sports

assessed May 30,2020, published 2016/06/04

Buckley John L.- 'People Don't Plan to Fail, they simply, Fail to Plan'

http: facebook.com/kendylife/photos/most people

John L. Buckley. assessed May 30, 2020, Daniel Kong, published 8/26/2019

III. Book:

Arnell, Peter *SHIFT, how to reinvent your business, your career and your personal brand & 2010*

Peter Arnell: "We can be the drivers of our destiny"-Page 199

Martha Stewart: "It's all about moving forward, not looking backward and changing for the better and forever"-Page Forward

Citation Continued

Webster's New College Dictionary, Riverside Edition II, Inspiration, 1984

Webster's New College Dictionary, Riverside Edition II, Need, 1984

Songs:

Earth, Wind & Fire, "Shining Star", B-Side, <u>That's The Way of The World</u>, Columbia,1975

George Benson," Greatest Love of All", B-Side, <u>The Greatest</u>, Arista Records, 1977

Ce Ce Winans," Pray" 3, <u>Purified</u>, Pure Springs Gospel, 2005

Bible Quotes

Romans 8:28

Romans 25:8

Romans 37:23

Luke 1:23

Matthew 5:16

Copyright Page:

King James Version, originally published in 1611, Red Letter Edition, Giant Print Reference Concordance, 1976 Thomas Nelson Publishers

Endnotes

1	John L. Buckley
2	M.B. Ray
3	Alana Stewart
4	Webster's Dictionary
5	Desmond Tutu
6	Tony Robbins
7	Desmond Tutu
8	Webster's Dictionary
9	Marcus Aurelius
10	Harriet Beecher Stowe
11	Anne Frank
12	Muhammad Ali
13	Russell Wilson
14	Peter Arnell
15	George Benson
16	CeCe Winan
17	Earth Wind & Fire
18	Francis of Assisi
19	Albert Einstein
20	Ralph Waldo Emerson
21	Helen Keller
22	Lou Holtz
23	Martha Stewart

CPSIA information can be obtained
at www.ICGtesting.com
Printed in the USA
BVHW030719250122
627016BV00017B/19